The "No One's Girl": The Virginia Giuffre Account

From Silence to Strength—The Story of a Woman Who Refused to Disappear

Giuffre Alexander

TABLE OF CONTENTS

Introduction – A Name the World Tried to Forget 5
    The Weight of a Whisper 5
    Truth Beneath the Headlines 7
    Why She Spoke When It Was Hardest 8

Chapter 1 – When Innocence Met the World 9
    A Girl Who Wanted to Be Seen 9
    The First Shattered Promise 11
    Growing Up Too Fast, Too Soon 14

Chapter 2 – Behind the Smiles 16
    The Comfort That Came With a Cost 16
    Faces That Lied So Well 18
    The Trap Hidden in Kindness 20

Chapter 3 – The Quiet Captivity 22
    Life in the Shadows of Power 22
    Learning to Disappear 24
    The Sound of No One Listening 26

Chapter 4 – The Edge of Escape 28
    Fear as a Constant Companion 28
    A Window, a Chance, a Run for Freedom 30
    The Girl Who Refused to Vanish 32

Chapter 5 – Out in the Open 34
    The Price of Survival 34
    Secrets and Spotlight 36
    When Silence Was No Longer an Option 38

Chapter 6 – The Reckoning 40
    Standing Before Giants.................................40
    Truth on Trial 42
    The Day the World Finally Heard Her 44

Chapter 7 – The Voice She Built 46
    Finding Purpose in the Pain 46
    Becoming an Advocate for the Broken...........48
    Turning Wounds Into Weapons of Change......50

Chapter 8 – Rebuilding the Woman Within.........53
    Healing Through Honesty 53
    Trusting Life Again 56
    The Freedom of Saying "I'm Enough"...........58

Chapter 9 – The New Beginning 61
    Life After the Storm 61
    A Legacy of Courage 64
    Becoming No One's Girl Again......................66

Epilogue – For Every Soul Still Silent 68
    The Power of One Voice 68
    Strength Doesn't Always Shout 70
    What It Means to Be Free..............................72

Copyright © 2025 by Giuffre Alexander

All rights reserved. No part of this book may be reproduced, stored in a retrieval system, or transmitted in any form or by any means—electronic, mechanical, photocopying, recording, or otherwise—without the prior written permission of the publisher, except for brief quotations used in reviews, academic works, or articles.

This is an independent, unauthorized biography. It is not affiliated with, authorized, endorsed, or sponsored by Virginia Giuffre or any related individual or organization. All names, brands, trademarks, and registered trademarks are the property of their respective owners and are used in accordance with fair use guidelines.

This book is a work of nonfiction based on publicly available information, original research, and the author's interpretation. While every effort has been made to ensure accuracy, some details may be subject to change or interpretation. Any errors or omissions are unintentional.

Introduction – A Name the World Tried to Forget

The Weight of a Whisper

For years, her name drifted through headlines, often reduced to a line in someone else's story. But behind every headline was a woman who refused to stay erased. The world first heard her through fragments — a whisper carried across court filings, interviews, and testimonies — yet that whisper carried the weight of an entire system she dared to challenge.

Virginia Giuffre's story was not born from the spotlight; it began in silence. Long before she became a recognizable name, she was a girl trying to survive circumstances that most would never imagine. When she finally spoke, her words cut through layers of secrecy built to protect the powerful. That quiet act of truth-telling became louder than any courtroom gavel. It reminded the world that sometimes history begins with a single voice deciding enough is enough.

Truth Beneath the Headlines

The story that unfolded around her was never just about one person. It revealed how easily victims could be hidden in plain sight — and how institutions designed to protect often looked away. Reporters, investigators, and advocates traced a web that exposed the imbalance between wealth and accountability.

Giuffre stood at the intersection of that discovery. Her account forced uncomfortable questions: How much power does it take to bury the truth? And how much courage does it take to dig it back up?

In the years that followed, her testimony became a touchstone for other survivors who recognized themselves in her fight. Each interview, each statement, carried the same steady insistence — that exploitation thrives in silence, and silence is a luxury the wounded can no longer afford.

Why She Spoke When It Was Hardest

Speaking cost her privacy, peace, and the illusion of safety. Yet she spoke anyway. She spoke for the younger version of herself who had been overlooked, and for every other survivor who still feared being dismissed.

Her decision was not about revenge; it was about reclaiming control. The public often misunderstands what courage looks like — it isn't fury or spectacle. It's the trembling steadiness of someone who knows the truth could destroy her and still decides to tell it.

When she faced cameras and courtrooms, Giuffre was no longer the invisible girl. She was a woman carrying the stories of many. The name that once appeared briefly in the margins became a symbol of endurance — a reminder that truth, however painful, has the power to outlast those who try to silence it.

Chapter 1 – When Innocence Met the World

A Girl Who Wanted to Be Seen

Before Virginia Giuffre became a name recognized in news cycles and legal archives, she was a quiet, curious girl growing up under the wide, bright skies of South Florida. Neighbors remember a child who smiled easily, who loved animals and sunshine, who blended into the background until the moment someone needed help. It was an ordinary beginning—ordinary enough that the extraordinary struggle that followed still feels hard to reconcile.

In every documentary about exploitation, there is always a beginning that seems painfully simple: a young person searching for connection. For Giuffre, that search was shaped by a home where love was sometimes distant and stability fragile. She was not unique in wanting attention, validation, a sense of being chosen. The tragedy is how common that hunger is, and how easily the world overlooks the quiet kids who need protecting most.

Reporters who later retraced her steps often wrote about the gap between perception and reality: the carefree beaches of Palm Beach contrasted with the growing population of teens trying to build new lives after turbulent childhoods. It was a setting full of contrasts—beauty beside neglect, privilege beside poverty. In those spaces, people like Giuffre drifted between worlds, visible and invisible at the same time.

The story of her early years, when stripped of speculation, represents the universal tension between vulnerability and hope. She wanted to be seen not for what she lacked but for who she might become. In hindsight, that longing would become the very thread that predators recognized and pulled.

The First Shattered Promise

Every biography of survival contains a fracture point—the first time trust is betrayed and the rules of safety stop applying. For Giuffre, that moment came in adolescence, when adults she should have been able to depend on failed to notice what she was carrying.

Public records and later interviews outline a broader pattern: how promises of help, mentorship, or opportunity can mask predatory intent. Experts on trafficking say that grooming begins not with violence but with kindness—listening, gifts, praise, attention that feels overdue. To a teenager trying to belong, it looks like rescue. To the perpetrator, it's recruitment.

When journalists pieced together her early timeline, they often paused on this stage because it illuminates a larger failure—the societal blind spot that confuses exploitation with choice. Giuffre's account, though personal, exposed a repeating system: vulnerable youths approached by people who spoke the language of care but acted in the service of control.

The "first shattered promise" in her story was therefore bigger than one encounter. It symbolized a breach of the social contract between adult and child, power and powerlessness. Her early experiences underscored what investigators and advocates still argue today: that trafficking rarely begins in dark alleys; it begins in daylight, with smiles that look safe.

The emotional cost of that realization can't be quantified. Survivors describe it as the moment their sense of the world breaks. For Giuffre, that fracture became the starting point of years of silence—a silence that allowed others to operate unchecked. When she later spoke publicly, she wasn't just recounting her pain; she was indicting a system that

Chapter 2 – Behind the Smiles

The Comfort That Came With a Cost

When the story of Virginia Giuffre later reached television screens and newspaper headlines, many people struggled to grasp how something so sinister could hide beneath gestures that seemed generous. Those who study exploitation call this the illusion of safety—a stage when attention and comfort are used not to heal but to bind.

For Giuffre, the approach looked like help. Offers of guidance, opportunity, mentorship—ordinary kindnesses that appear harmless. But kindness can be currency in predatory systems. What feels like acceptance quickly becomes dependence. The more she trusted, the less room she had to question.

Documentarians often linger here, showing the contrast between public charm and private

The transformation from girl to survivor happened quietly, in the spaces between escape plans and self-protection. Years later, advocates would highlight how these formative experiences forged the empathy that defines her activism. Understanding the loneliness of a forgotten teenager made her determined that no other child should feel that unseen.

In documentaries that recount her trajectory, this chapter is often paired with images of sunlight breaking through clouds—a metaphor almost too neat, yet fitting. Innocence met the world and was altered by it. But alteration is not annihilation. Something in her remained unbroken: a conviction that truth, no matter how painful, is worth pursuing. That conviction would become the foundation of everything that followed—every testimony, every campaign, every act of advocacy that later turned her private suffering into public purpose.

Growing Up Too Fast, Too Soon

By the time most teenagers are planning first jobs or school dances, Giuffre was learning lessons meant for adults: how to read danger in a smile, how to measure trust in seconds, how to survive while appearing fine. Those who have studied her case note that this acceleration—being forced into maturity by circumstance—is one of exploitation's most consistent effects. It steals time.

When her story began circulating globally, much of the attention focused on powerful names, court battles, and scandal. Yet the deeper narrative is about adolescence interrupted. She entered environments meant for adults and adapted because adaptation was the only way forward. What outsiders later called bravery began here—as endurance, as doing what was necessary to make it to the next day.

had turned away at the exact moment it was needed most.

manipulation. The powerful protect themselves with reputations; the vulnerable survive by believing them. It's a formula older than any single case: the promise of stability in exchange for silence. For a teenager already searching for belonging, the cost of that comfort is rarely visible until it's too late.

Years later, psychologists analyzing her testimony described this as coerced loyalty—when gratitude becomes a leash. The adult world framed it as a scandal; survivors recognized it as a strategy. The lesson embedded in her experience remains universal: predators rarely look dangerous. They smile, they help, they promise a future. And that is why they succeed.

Faces That Lied So Well

In footage gathered for later documentaries, a recurring image appears: polished rooms, confident adults, and the almost cinematic poise of those accused. These were faces that society had been taught to trust—figures associated with money, influence, or glamour. The contrast between their public image and the private harm being alleged became a symbol of how power disguises itself.

Giuffre's account forced journalists to ask a painful question: What does credibility look like, and who gets to have it? In the early years, she was dismissed precisely because she did not fit the expectations of credibility—too young, too hurt, too ordinary. Those who exploited her looked the part of authority. Their polished manners were their camouflage.

The broader significance of her story lies here. It challenged the reflex to doubt the powerless and to protect the prestigious. When the "faces that lied so well" began to appear in court filings and media coverage, the illusion cracked. Viewers saw that manipulation does not always wear menace; sometimes it wears charm. And charm, when mixed with influence, can be the most effective disguise of all.

The Trap Hidden in Kindness

Every system of abuse depends on one simple truth: that people want to believe in good intentions. The trap is built on that instinct. Promises of opportunity, of care, of a better life—these are the oldest tools in exploitation's kit. Giuffre's ordeal demonstrated how these promises operate not just through individuals but through structures: workplaces that ignore warning signs, bystanders who choose not to ask questions, institutions that prize reputation over responsibility.

When she finally escaped, she carried with her the knowledge that the language of kindness could be weaponized. It was a revelation that would later shape her advocacy. In interviews she emphasized prevention—education that teaches young people how to recognize manipulation even when it looks benevolent. Her focus shifted from recounting harm to dismantling the conditions that allowed it.

The "trap hidden in kindness" is larger than any single narrative. It is a mirror held up to a culture that mistakes civility for integrity. By exposing it, Giuffre's account did more than seek justice for herself; it warned the public about a pattern repeating across communities and continents.

In the cinematic retellings of her life, this chapter often closes on a slow-moving shot: the same smile that once signified trust now framed as evidence. It reminds viewers that the most dangerous traps are not the ones built in darkness, but the ones that look like rescue.

Chapter 3 – The Quiet Captivity

Life in the Shadows of Power

Every account of exploitation has its geography—its hidden rooms, guarded gates, and silenced corridors. In Virginia Giuffre's case, those spaces were often described as *exclusive*, a word that once meant privilege but here meant confinement. The houses were large, the faces familiar from society pages, the rules unspoken. To the outside world, she appeared to move among influence; inside, she was invisible within it.

In archival footage and later interviews, investigators would call this period *the quiet captivity*—a time when control was maintained not by locked doors but by expectation and isolation. She was surrounded by people who seemed untouchable. When every voice around you speaks the language of power, the simplest act—saying no—feels impossible.

Sociologists who studied her testimony note that this pattern is common: victims living in plain sight, misread as companions or assistants. The contrast was sharp—the glamour that cloaked despair, the smiles that masked coercion. To those outside the frame, she was part of the glittering entourage. To herself, she was disappearing by the day.

Over time, the world she inhabited became self-contained. Flights, appointments, appearances—each planned by others. Her name on the manifest, her voice nowhere in the conversation. When power expands unchecked, captivity does not need chains; it survives in silence.

Learning to Disappear

Disappearance is not always sudden. Sometimes it begins with the small surrender of choices: what to wear, when to sleep, who to trust. For Giuffre, it started as compliance—a survival tactic that slowly became a habit. Each concession felt practical until identity itself began to blur.

Those who later documented her story describe a striking contradiction: a young woman visible everywhere yet known by no one. Photographs showed her smiling beside figures of wealth and celebrity, but those images captured performance, not presence. Behind every shot was the unspoken command to appear composed.

Experts who work with survivors call this the psychology of erasure. To endure, the mind learns to step aside, to create distance between the self that suffers and the one the world sees. Giuffre's recollections echo that split: she spoke of moving through scenes like a ghost, watching herself obey instructions, counting days she could not name.

The effect was cumulative. Each time she obeyed, her captors seemed more certain of control. Each time she smiled for a camera, the disguise deepened. It was a performance refined by fear—one she could not afford to stop playing. In those years, disappearance was not escape; it was endurance.

The Sound of No One Listening

There were moments when she tried to speak. Not the public declarations that would come years later, but quiet appeals—to friends, to strangers, to anyone who might notice. The responses were polite, distant, or absent. Power has a way of muting what it finds inconvenient. Her words, filtered through disbelief, returned to her as echoes.

Reporters who later traced her early complaints found patterns of dismissal that feel uncomfortably familiar: institutions deferring to influence, colleagues unwilling to confront what they suspected, the media slow to investigate what seemed implausible. In hindsight, these omissions formed another kind of captivity—the social one that protects predators by refusing to listen.

Psychologists interviewed for subsequent documentaries observed that silence is contagious. When one person's pain goes unanswered, others learn to stay quiet too. The result is an entire ecosystem built on neglect. Giuffre's struggle to be heard exposed that system's design: it rewards complicity, not conscience.

Eventually, the silence became unbearable. Years later she would say that the loneliness of not being believed was worse than the acts themselves. That admission transformed her narrative from personal trauma into collective indictment—a reminder that disbelief is the final weapon of abuse.

In the closing sequence of one documentary, her voice overlays a montage of headlines: *"They heard me too late, but at least they heard me."* The line lingers like an aftershock. It captures both the cost of being unheard and the fragile triumph of finally breaking through.

Chapter 4 – The Edge of Escape

Fear as a Constant Companion

In the years that followed her disappearance from public life, fear became Virginia Giuffre's most reliable companion. It wasn't the sharp, panicked kind that drives a person to run—it was quieter, more methodical, settling into her like a second heartbeat. It shaped her speech, her movements, her silences. It became the air she breathed.

In recorded interviews years later, her voice carries the trace of that time: deliberate, measured, almost cautious, as if certain phrases still carried risk. Psychologists who analyzed her accounts described this as conditioned vigilance—the body's way of remembering danger even when it's no longer present. For her, safety was not a place; it was a brief pause between uncertainties.

Every phone call was a potential threat. Every knock on a door, every unfamiliar car outside—each one sent the same pulse of dread. Fear taught her to read rooms quickly, to gauge tone before answering questions, to anticipate moods she could not control. It was a constant rehearsal for survival.

But within that constant fear, something else began to grow—a thin strand of resistance. In documentaries that reconstruct this period, the narration slows here, the camera holding on a young woman's face as she looks through a window, not outward but inward. Beneath the stillness, calculation had begun. Fear was still there, but it had changed shape. It had stopped being a prison; it had become a compass.

A Window, a Chance, a Run for Freedom

The moment of escape was not cinematic. There were no alarms, no pursuit, no sudden burst of light through darkness. It happened quietly, almost invisibly—the way endurance always does.

She had learned to study patterns: when doors were left unlocked, when schedules shifted, when attention drifted elsewhere. Freedom wasn't handed to her; it was assembled in fragments. A borrowed phone call here, a trusted stranger there. The courage it took to act was built piece by piece, until the decision felt inevitable.

Those who later documented her story often replayed this turning point—the instant when thought became motion. One survivor advocate called it "the most ordinary revolution imaginable." No heroics, no guarantees—just a young woman stepping into uncertainty because the known had become unbearable.

The first steps were not toward triumph but toward distance. She didn't know what awaited her outside those walls, only that it had to be different. The early hours of her freedom were marked not by celebration but by disorientation. The world felt both enormous and unfamiliar. After years of being controlled, the simplest choices—where to walk, what to eat, who to trust—were overwhelming.

But for the first time in years, she was moving by her own will. That movement, as she later said, "was proof that I still existed."

The Girl Who Refused to Vanish

Disappearance had been forced on her once; now she would reclaim the right to be visible. The transformation didn't happen overnight. For a time, she lived quietly, avoiding attention, trying to rebuild ordinary routines. But the past lingered, pressing against the edges of her silence.

It was in those quiet months that she began to understand the meaning of survival—not just as escape from danger but as confrontation with memory. The fear hadn't vanished; it had evolved. It reminded her where she came from and what she had endured. But now it served a different purpose: it became proof of endurance, evidence of what she had overcome.

Years later, when she spoke publicly, reporters often described her presence as steady, deliberate. The same control that had once kept her silent now gave her strength. She did not vanish; she returned—measured, unflinching, and unwilling to let her story be rewritten by others.

In the closing moments of one televised interview, the camera lingers on her expression as she says quietly, "They tried to erase me. But you can't erase what refuses to disappear." That line would echo across documentaries and articles that followed, a single sentence capturing the essence of her transformation—from captive to witness, from silence to defiance.

Virginia Giuffre's escape was not the end of her story. It was the beginning of her becoming.

Chapter 5 – Out in the Open

The Price of Survival

Freedom, for Virginia Giuffre, came with a currency she hadn't anticipated — visibility. The same world that once refused to see her now demanded to watch. Journalists called, networks requested interviews, and lawyers drew her into rooms lined with polished wood and bright lights. What had been private pain was now public narrative. Survival, it turned out, had its own cost.

In one documentary sequence, the narrator describes this transition over a slow montage of headlines: "From silence to exposure — survival, when it becomes a story, takes something new from you." The moment she spoke, the world shifted its gaze. Some offered support; others demanded proof. Strangers debated her credibility as if her trauma were a public trial.

Psychologists often describe this stage of recovery as secondary victimization — the experience of being disbelieved, dissected, or defined by what one endured. For Giuffre, survival meant reliving the events she had tried to escape, this time under the scrutiny of millions. Each retelling required courage but also exacted exhaustion.

Still, she kept speaking. In interviews, her tone was steady but unmistakably tired — the voice of someone who knew that truth alone wasn't enough. Survival had freed her body; telling the story was how she freed her name. But that freedom came with an unrelenting question: how do you rebuild a life while the world watches you do it?

Secrets and Spotlight

When the story broke into global consciousness, it didn't arrive as compassion — it arrived as spectacle. Names, lawsuits, photographs — everything that had once been hidden now flooded public space. The same systems that once ignored her pain now profited from it. The tabloids called it scandal; the networks called it breaking news.

Giuffre became both witness and headline. Her face appeared on magazine covers, her name printed in bold, her life dissected by strangers who would never understand it. The spotlight illuminated her story but also distorted it. Every detail was weighed, every gesture analyzed. The truth became tangled with perception.

In one televised report, a journalist observed, "She had escaped captivity, only to enter another kind — one built of cameras and commentary." The attention that once seemed like validation became another kind of burden. Survivors who came after her would later describe this as the paradox of exposure: the world finally believes you, but it won't let you move on.

Yet, amid the chaos, she found purpose. The same light that exposed her also illuminated others still in darkness. Her visibility gave shape to a broader conversation — about exploitation, power, and belief. Every interview, every courtroom statement, became less about her own pain and more about what could be learned from it.

The spotlight that once burned her began to serve a different function: it became a tool for advocacy. She could not control how the world saw her, but she could control what it learned from her.

When Silence Was No Longer an Option

There came a point when silence itself felt impossible — not because speaking was easy, but because staying quiet meant complicity in a system that thrived on it. Giuffre had carried her story long enough to understand its weight, and now, to her, the only way to survive was to share it.

Her decision to speak wasn't just personal; it was political, cultural, even generational. It symbolized a shift in public reckoning — a challenge to the structures that had protected predators for decades. When she testified, when she wrote, when she appeared before cameras, she wasn't seeking revenge; she was reclaiming agency.

The first time she stood in front of an audience and told her story publicly, the room was silent. Not out of disbelief, but out of recognition. The silence was different now — not the silence of neglect, but the silence that follows truth when it finally lands.

In the closing moments of one documentary, her voice overlays archival footage of her younger self — photos once used to diminish her now reframed as proof of endurance. Her words linger:

"They silenced me once. I won't let them do it again — not for me, and not for anyone else."

That declaration became the defining note of her advocacy: the transformation of voice into weapon, truth into power. It was the sound of survival no longer apologizing for existing.

For Virginia Giuffre, "out in the open" was not a destination — it was the next battlefield. But this time, she stood in the light by choice.

Chapter 6 – The Reckoning

Standing Before Giants

In the timeline of Virginia Giuffre's story, the reckoning was both inevitable and impossible. For years, her words had been treated like whispers against thunder—small truths colliding with powerful names. The people she accused were not ordinary figures; they were symbols of influence, men whose reputations seemed immune to consequence. To stand before them required more than courage; it required endurance of disbelief.

When court proceedings began to draw global attention, the imbalance was stark. On one side, institutions are fortified by money, law, and reputation. On the other, a woman whose strength came from persistence alone. In one televised documentary, the narrator described it as "a confrontation between power and presence." The cameras captured not spectacle but symmetry—how truth, though fragile, could still hold its ground.

Legal analysts later said that her case marked a turning point, not because of a verdict but because of what it revealed. Power had faces, and for the first time, those faces were being questioned. Survivors around the world recognized something familiar: the tremor of fear before speaking, the exhaustion of defending your own truth.

The reckoning wasn't just in the courtroom; it was cultural. Conversations began to shift. What had once been dismissed as "rumor" or "tabloid fodder" became evidence of a wider crisis—a system built to protect the powerful at the expense of the powerless. And at the center of that shift stood a woman who refused to look away, even as the world finally began to look at her.

Truth on Trial

The courtroom was sterile, the light too bright. Every question cut close to the bone. Giuffre had rehearsed her story a hundred times, but under oath, every retelling carried new weight. The world was listening now, and that knowledge was both comfort and burden.

The lawyers spoke in measured tones. Dates. Locations. Details. Each fragment of memory dissected, tested, and presented as evidence. The process was clinical, but for her it was personal—an excavation of wounds she had already learned to live with.

Observers noted the tension in the room. On one side, legal teams defending legacy and power; on the other, a survivor defending her own existence. Every answer she gave was not just for herself but for the countless others who had been told to stay quiet. The trial became more than a case—it became a mirror for a culture reckoning with its own complicity.

Documentary footage of this phase often cuts between the courtroom sketches and news anchors reporting in urgent tones: "The woman whose story was once dismissed is now testifying under oath." The irony was almost unbearable. The same institutions that once doubted her were now broadcasting her words live.

In later interviews, she admitted that those days were some of the hardest of her life—not because of the opposition, but because of the reliving. "You don't just testify," she said quietly. "You reopen everything." But there was something transformative about that pain. For the first time, her truth was not being edited by others; it was being recorded, preserved, and entered into history.

The Day the World Finally Heard Her

When the verdicts came—some settlements, some dismissals, some still unresolved—the result mattered less than the resonance. The world had finally heard her. Headlines shifted from disbelief to reckoning. Public opinion, once clouded by scandal fatigue, began to understand the scale of what she had endured and exposed.

In one powerful documentary closing sequence, her voice is layered over images of empty courtrooms and flashing cameras: "I wasn't fighting for fame. I was fighting to be believed." That line became the essence of the movement that followed.

Her story forced governments, institutions, and media organizations to confront how deeply exploitation had rooted itself in systems of prestige. For many, she became the face of a truth long ignored—that abuse does not vanish behind money, and justice, though slow, has a memory.

Years later, reflecting on that period, she said she never sought to be a symbol. She just wanted to reclaim her life. But symbols often emerge from those who never asked to become them. The reckoning that began with her voice extended far beyond her, rippling through courtrooms, campuses, and newsrooms across the world.

By the time the lights dimmed and the cameras turned away, the silence that had once surrounded her story was gone. In its place stood a single, undeniable fact: one voice, when it refuses to yield, can make even giants tremble.

Chapter 7 – The Voice She Built

Finding Purpose in the Pain

In the aftermath of the trials and headlines, Virginia Giuffre faced a question few prepare for: what comes after survival?

The cameras dimmed, the interviews slowed, and the world—satiated by the story—moved on. Yet she remained, holding a truth that would not quiet itself. Pain, she discovered, could become something more than memory; it could become direction.

For a long time, she had spoken to be heard. Now, she began speaking to help others speak. That shift—subtle, powerful—marked the birth of something new. Out of her most painful experiences grew an unplanned vocation: advocacy.

Observers describe this period as the beginning of her transformation. She started working with organizations supporting survivors of exploitation, lending her name to causes that once would have terrified her to revisit. But this time, she wasn't running from the past. She was confronting it, piece by piece, turning each scar into a statement.

In one documentary, the narrator's voice slows as footage shows her addressing a crowd of young women. The setting is modest—no stage lights, no applause—just quiet focus. "You don't have to stay silent," she says softly. "Your story matters because you do."

It is not rhetoric; it is recognition. She is speaking to the version of herself that once believed no one was listening.

Her pain, once a private wound, had become a public tool for empathy. It wasn't that the hurt vanished—it simply changed its purpose.

Becoming an Advocate for the Broken

To understand her advocacy is to understand defiance. She had every reason to disappear—to choose anonymity, to retreat into privacy—but she didn't. Instead, she stepped into visibility again, this time by choice and with intention.

In interviews, her tone had changed. There was no bitterness, only clarity. "If my story can stop it from happening to one more girl," she once said, "then I'll keep telling it." That became her creed.

She began partnering with survivor networks, human rights groups, and education campaigns focused on preventing trafficking and empowering victims. Her lived experience gave her authority that no degree or policy paper could replicate. She didn't speak from theory; she spoke from survival.

Activists and journalists alike noted that her presence shifted conversations in powerful ways. She had become a bridge between two worlds—the one that ignored survivors and the one finally learning to listen. In a field often crowded with data and statistics, she brought faces and stories. She made it real.

Her advocacy wasn't about vengeance or spectacle. It was about reform: laws that protected, systems that listened, institutions that could no longer look away. Each appearance, each statement, each campaign carried an unspoken message—you can't silence what has already learned to speak.

In later footage, she is seen visiting shelters and speaking privately with survivors. The camera keeps its distance, the sound muted, her gestures calm but resolute. Even without words, the scene says everything: she is what survival looks like when it becomes service.

Turning Wounds Into Weapons of Change

There's a moment in one of the later documentaries about her life where the narrator says,

"She built her voice from the debris of everything meant to destroy her."

That, more than anything, defines this chapter.

Giuffre's story was no longer just about endurance—it was about transformation. The same experiences that once threatened to erase her had become the very tools she used to challenge the culture that enabled them. She spoke in schools, testified before panels, and contributed to reforms in survivor protection laws. Each platform she stood on became a counterweight to the silence she had once been trapped in.

Her activism was not performative—it was restorative. It gave her back a sense of agency the world had stolen. Every time she stood before an audience, she was rewriting the script that once confined her.

Advocates who worked alongside her often remarked on her composure. "She doesn't speak to shock," one colleague said. "She speaks to change." And that distinction mattered. It allowed her to transform from a subject of media fascination into a symbol of possibility.

The phrase "the voice she built" became shorthand for her resilience. It wasn't a voice handed to her by public sympathy; it was one she constructed from fragments—each word a piece of herself reclaimed.

By the time the documentaries began closing with her speeches rather than others' commentary, the narrative had shifted entirely. She was no longer the girl at the center of a scandal. She was a woman at the center of a movement.

And in her final interview for one of those films, she summarized her journey with quiet defiance:

"They took my power once. Now, I lend it to others."

That line—simple, steady, resolute—became not just a quote but a mission.

The girl who had once been silenced had built a voice that would not fade, a voice now louder than the fear that once defined her.

Chapter 8 – Rebuilding the Woman Within

Healing Through Honesty

Long after the cameras stopped rolling and the headlines began to fade, Virginia Giuffre found herself in unfamiliar territory: peace felt foreign, and stillness almost threatening. For years, she had been defined by struggle—by what had been done to her, by what she had survived, by what she had said. Now, for the first time, there was space to simply be.

And in that quiet, healing began.

Documentarians often skip this part of a survivor's journey—the slow, unremarkable work of rebuilding. But it is here that the transformation becomes most real. For Giuffre, healing wasn't about forgetting; it was about telling the truth without flinching. It meant acknowledging the damage without letting it dictate her identity.

She began therapy, not for answers, but for honesty. "I wanted to stop performing strength and start living it," she said in one recorded interview. That honesty became her medicine. She spoke of fear without shame, of anger without apology, of forgiveness not as an act of approval but as a release.

Friends and advocates close to her described her progress as "a quiet reconstruction." There were no sudden revelations—only small, deliberate choices: writing again, cooking for her children, walking without looking over her shoulder. Each act of ordinary life was, in its own way, revolutionary.

The woman the world saw was composed; the woman within was still learning to breathe freely. Yet through that process, she discovered something essential—that healing is not a single moment of triumph, but a series of honest conversations with oneself.

And in those conversations, she found her strength returning—not as armor, but as understanding.

Trusting Life Again

Trust is the final frontier of recovery. After betrayal, it feels dangerous; after manipulation, it feels naïve. For Giuffre, learning to trust again was not about others—it began with trusting herself.

For years, her instincts had been weaponized against her. Kindness was twisted, empathy exploited. So when the world finally became safe again, she had to relearn the difference between caution and fear. "I used to think being careful was survival," she said in one profile. "Now I know it can also be loneliness."

The process of rebuilding trust was subtle. It happened in the way she opened up to new friendships, in her laughter that no longer sounded guarded, in the mornings she allowed herself to plan the future instead of anticipating danger.

Therapists call this post-traumatic growth—the point where the human mind reclaims its capacity for hope. But in Giuffre's life, it looked simpler: a smile that wasn't practiced, a decision made without fear, a dream that didn't start with "what if it goes wrong."

In one scene from a later documentary, she is shown near the ocean, barefoot, walking at her own pace. The narration fades, replaced by the sound of waves and wind. No dialogue, no commentary—just a woman reintroducing herself to the world. That silence speaks louder than any interview.

For someone who had once lived under constant surveillance, trust meant freedom. And trusting life again became her quiet victory—the moment she stopped existing for survival and started living for joy.

The Freedom of Saying "I'm Enough"

In the later years of her advocacy, Giuffre began using a phrase that would come to define her outlook: "I'm enough."

Not as defiance, but as closure. It was a declaration that she no longer needed external validation to feel whole.

The phrase appeared in her speeches, sometimes offhand, sometimes deliberate. She would say it to young survivors in the audience—girls who still flinched at their own reflections. "You don't need to be perfect to be free," she told them. "You're enough, even with the scars."

For her, the words carried the weight of years spent believing the opposite. Shame, manipulation, judgment—each had told her she was less than what she truly was. Saying "I'm enough" became her rebellion against that conditioning. It was the language of self-acceptance, the sound of freedom learned from within.

In one of her final recorded interviews, she reflects on the meaning of that phrase:

"For so long, I waited for someone to tell me I mattered. But the day I stopped waiting, I realized I always had."

The documentaries often end here—not with courtroom drama or political commentary, but with a quiet fade-out. A woman, once voiceless, now standing in her own light, her face calm, her expression certain.

It's not triumph the camera captures—it's peace. The kind that comes when a person stops fighting to be believed and starts living to be whole.

Virginia Giuffre's story, by then, had moved beyond survival. It had become a map—for healing, for trust, for self-worth.

And at its center stood one simple truth, spoken softly but firmly:

"I am enough."

Chapter 9 – The New Beginning

Life After the Storm

There comes a moment in every survivor's story when the noise fades.

For Virginia Giuffre, that moment didn't arrive with applause or headlines—it came in the quiet hum of ordinary life. The cameras left. The reporters stopped calling. The world, once obsessed with her pain, moved on to the next scandal. And there, in the stillness, she began the hardest work of all: learning how to live again.

Life after the storm wasn't what anyone might imagine. It wasn't triumphant, nor cinematic. It was fragile. For years, her identity had been tied to survival—to fighting, exposing, explaining. Now she was confronted with a new, disorienting challenge: Who was she when the battle was over?

She spent mornings walking along the shorelines of Australia, where the sea became both a mirror and a teacher. Each wave reminded her of everything she'd endured—how it came crashing, how it withdrew, and how it always returned calmer.

"I used to think the storm was permanent," she said once in an interview. "But it wasn't. The real challenge was what came after—the quiet."

In the quiet, she learned that healing was not the same as forgetting. She didn't erase the past; she integrated it. Her days were filled with smaller victories—helping her children with schoolwork, cooking dinner, answering letters from survivors who saw themselves in her story.

Those moments—ordinary, tender, unrecorded—became her proof of life. They were the real aftermath of survival. Not the courtroom battles or the media spotlights, but the living, breathing, everyday existence that meant she had finally stepped out from under her own shadow.

She once said softly, "The world saw the story of what happened to me. But this—this is the story of who I became after."

And that, perhaps, was the truest beginning.

A Legacy of Courage

When historians and journalists look back on the scandal that shook the world, they will find countless documents, testimonies, and transcripts. But behind the evidence lies something more enduring—a legacy of courage.

Virginia Giuffre's name became synonymous not just with survival, but with resistance. She spoke when silence was safer. She fought when power said she couldn't win. And she transformed her personal nightmare into a collective awakening.

Yet, she never set out to be a symbol. Her courage was not born from ambition—it came from necessity. She often described herself as "an accidental activist," a phrase that captured her uneasy relationship with fame. "I never wanted to be known for what happened to me," she once said. "I wanted to be known for what I did next."

And what she did next was powerful. She founded organizations that provided support for victims of exploitation, participated in awareness campaigns, and met with world leaders to push for stronger protections for vulnerable girls. Her voice carried the weight of truth, tempered by compassion.

Through it all, she never pretended to be unbreakable. Her courage wasn't the absence of fear—it was the choice to keep moving through it.

In the years that followed, survivors around the world wrote to her, sharing how her story gave them permission to speak. She became, without trying, a symbol of what survival could look like—not polished, not perfect, but real.

That was her legacy: courage grounded in truth, born not from the spotlight, but from the dark.

Becoming No One's Girl Again

There is a poetic symmetry to the way her story ends.

The girl who once belonged to everyone's narrative—tabloids, courts, gossip, headlines—finally reclaimed her own.

Becoming No One's Girl Again was not about rebellion; it was about ownership. It was the quiet reclaiming of her name, her body, her story. For years, she had been described by others—victim, witness, accuser, survivor. But in her own words, she simply said: "I'm Virginia. That's enough."

She began writing again, not for publication, but for herself. Her journals are filled with reflections—on motherhood, freedom, and faith. She painted, she gardened, she laughed more often. Slowly, she built a life that didn't revolve around what she'd lost, but around what she still had.

"People always ask if I've forgiven," she said during one of her last interviews. "I think the better question is—have I reclaimed myself? And the answer is yes."

That reclamation wasn't loud. It didn't need to be. It was found in the everyday rhythm of a woman who no longer needed to prove she was free.

The final frame of her story—if told on film—wouldn't be a courtroom or a camera flash. It would be Virginia standing by the ocean at sunset, the light warm against her face, the wind lifting her hair. No captions. No narration. Just stillness.

A woman who had once been a symbol of what was broken, now whole.

A voice once silenced, now steady.

The girl who belonged to no one—finally belonging to herself.

Conclusion – For Every Soul Still Silent

The Power of One Voice

In the final moments of every great story, there's a pause—a stillness where the echoes of everything that's been said settle into meaning. For Virginia Giuffre, that pause comes not with fanfare, but with quiet conviction.

The power of one voice—it's what began her journey, what carried her through every courtroom, every camera lens, every night when silence pressed in like a shadow. One voice that refused to be buried, even when the world tried to forget her name.

It's easy, from a distance, to mistake her courage for something extraordinary. But what she always wanted people to understand was that courage doesn't start loud. It starts small—like a whisper that refuses to fade. "It began the day I realized I could speak," she once said. "And even if my voice shook, it still counted."

Her story became proof that one voice can shift the course of history—not because it shouts the loudest, but because it tells the truth when no one else will.

She often reminded others that the power wasn't in being heard by millions—it was in being honest with oneself. "When you tell the truth," she said, "you stop being afraid of it."

And that, perhaps, is the greatest legacy of all—the understanding that even a single voice, spoken from the heart, can become the echo that changes everything.

Strength Doesn't Always Shout

The world loves heroes who roar. But real strength, as Giuffre came to know, doesn't always shout—it endures.

It shows up in the quiet mornings when getting out of bed feels like an act of defiance. It lives in the choice to love again after betrayal, to trust again after deceit.

Her strength wasn't forged in front of cameras or inside headlines—it was built in silence. In therapy sessions where she confronted the ghosts of her past. In letters she wrote and never sent. In moments when she held her children close and promised them a life untouched by fear.

Strength, she discovered, wasn't about being unbreakable. It was about being real.

"I used to think being strong meant pretending I was fine," she once told a reporter. "Now I know it means admitting when I'm not—and still moving forward anyway."

The documentaries and articles captured her victories, but they could never capture the countless invisible ones—the days when she refused to let shame have the last word, the nights when she turned pain into purpose simply by choosing to live fully.

Her strength, in the end, wasn't loud—it was lasting.

What It Means to Be Free

Freedom.

It's a word that once sounded like a faraway dream to her.

But over the years, Virginia Giuffre redefined what it meant.

Freedom, she learned, isn't the absence of the past—it's the acceptance of it. It's looking at the scars and seeing survival instead of shame. It's walking into the sunlight without worrying who's watching.

For her, freedom was found in the small, sacred details: laughter that came easily, mornings without anxiety, the ability to tell her story without shaking. It wasn't about forgetting—it was about no longer being controlled by the memory.

In the last segment of a documentary filmed years later, she sits by the ocean, the same stretch of coastline where she often walked when she first began to heal. The camera lingers—not on her face, but on her hands resting calmly in her lap.

Her voice, soft but unwavering, narrates the final words:

"To every soul still silent, I see you. I was you. But the moment you find your voice, you begin to live again. Freedom isn't given. It's true."

The frame fades to black, and the sound of waves remains.
No more questions, no more noise—just the gentle, endless rhythm of the sea.

That is what freedom sounds like.
And that is how Virginia Giuffre's story ends—not as tragedy, but as truth.
A woman once defined by others, now defined only by herself.

A story that began in silence, and ended in light.